The IN AMERICA *Series*

THE CZECHS AND SLOVAKS
IN AMERICA

JOSEPH S. ROUCEK, Ph. D.

*Professor and Head of the
Departments of Political
Science and Sociology
(Retired)*

University of Bridgeport,
Connecticut

Published by
Lerner Publications Company
Minneapolis, Minnesota

To my beloved friends,
Vincent and Theresa Weston
of Bridgeport, Connecticut

Second Printing 1968

Copyright © 1967 by Lerner Publications Company

International Copyright Secured. Printed in U.S.A.

Library of Congress Catalog Card Number: 67-15685

. . . CONTENTS . . .

Prague, May 1945. Citizens gather in the main square near the John Hus monument to watch Soviet troops march by. Six years of Nazi rule in Czechoslovakia ended when American and Russian armies liberated the country.

PART I

European Background

1. Who Are the Czechs?

The average American of Czechoslovakian background is more or less accustomed to having his neighbors and friends refer to Czechoslovakia as a new country, formed only in 1918. He is also used to having his group, as immigrants, classified as new immigrants. Yet Czechoslovakia's history goes back to the fifth century A.D., and Czech immigrants settled in America as early as the colonial period.

The history of the Czech people is difficult to understand. This difficulty is increased when the Czechs are called Bohemians, Moravians, or the Slavish people. In America, the words "Slavs" and "Slavish" are often used to classify immigrants from Central, Eastern, and Balkan Europe. At one time they covered all non-English speaking peoples, even Italians.

Who are the Slavs? There is, strictly speaking, no such person as a Slav. Instead, the term is used to describe a number of nationalities that are bound together by ties of blood, culture, and language. The largest and most important nationalities that make up the Slavic peoples are:

Russians (Great Russians and White Russians)
Ukrainians (Little Russians and Ruthenians)
Poles
Czechs (Bohemians and Moravians)
Slovaks
Yugoslavs (Serbs, Croats, Slovenes)
Bulgarians

Thus, the Slavs represent a group of distinct nations, each with its own literature, history, and culture. In America they have different churches, societies, newspapers, and a separate social life. But there is sometimes a feeling among these people that they belong to a single Slavonic group of nations. Some Slavs feel this tie much more than others. Nevertheless, there is a striking similarity in the way of life in rural districts of the various Slavic countries. The Slavic languages, too, are clearly related to one another.

The Czechs, who number among the Slav people, are often called Bohemians. The word "Bohemia" refers to the westernmost province of Czechoslovakia. Its name was derived from the Boii, the people who occupied or claimed parts of the region before the Christian era. During the time of the Holy Roman Empire, Bohemia was recognized by the emperors as an independent kingdom, settled by Czechs. Thus, the Czechs are often referred to as Bohemians. They also are called Moravians, since they occupied Moravia as well as the neighboring territories of Silesia and Slovakia.

Karluv Tyn Castle in Bohemia, built by King Charles IV in 1348.

Charles University Library, Prague. This school, founded by Charles IV in 1348, is the oldest university in Central Europe.

2. Czechoslovakia ... the Beginning

The early history of the Czech people is somewhat unclear. It is believed, however, that they came from southern Russia and settled in Bohemia and Moravia sometime before 500 A.D. According to national legends, the first Bohemian to reach the area that is now Prague was called Cech. His descendants were named Cechs or Czechs.

In the ninth century the pagan Czechs accepted Christianity. The various tribes became united under native kings. The Czechs reached an important position among the European nations. They ruled, in turn, over Hungary, Poland, and Galicia. By the end of the century, however, the Czechs living in Slovakia were conquered by the Magyars, a people of Hungary. This step had tremendous historical importance. For about 1,000 years Slovakia remained under the control of the Empire of Austria and after 1867 under Austria-Hungary, thus separated from Bohemia.

King Charles IV (1316-1378) became Holy Roman Emperor in 1347. The king of Bohemia had been one of the seven electors of the Empire since the thirteenth century, but Charles made the Bohemian electorship more secure. Under him Prague became the ruling center of the Empire, which at that time consisted of Bohemia, the German states, and small portions of the Netherlands, France, and Italy.

In the thirteenth century another fateful historical incident took place. The Bohemian rulers invited German colonists to settle in the border regions of Bohemia in order to stimulate trade and industry. These immigrants built towns and were allowed to enclose their settlements with walls and to administer law independently of the Bohemian law courts.

During the fourteenth century, education, art, and architecture in Bohemia thrived under King Charles IV, known as the "father of his country." He founded Charles University in Prague in 1348, the first university in Central Europe and one which still exists today.

3. *John Hus and the Hussite Wars*

In the fifteenth century a great national and religious leader arose in the person of John Hus, the rector of Charles University and a famous preacher. Hus preached to the Czechs in their own language instead of Latin, the official language of the Church. Like many other reformers of his time, he was angered by the abuses within the Church. Eventually he was excommunicated for his views.

Hus decided to present his ideas of reform before the Council of Constance in Switzerland in 1415. He was guaranteed a safe journey and return by the Holy Roman Emperor himself. However, Hus's views were not heard by the council. Instead, he was thrown into prison, tried as a heretic, and later burned at the stake. He is still honored by the Czech people as the first religious (Protestant) reformer of Central Europe. Hus had great confidence in the final victory of truth, a confidence which was expressed in the motto afterwards adopted by his followers: "Pravda vitezi"— "The truth will win!" This became the motto of the Czechoslovak Republic.

The burning of John Hus at the stake was followed by the Hussite Wars, which lasted nearly 60 years. The loyal followers of Hus fought off army after army sent by the Holy Roman Emperor. The Czechs were aroused, and the whole country declared its loyalty to the Hussite cause.

John Hus (1369?-1415), a religious reformer whose teachings became part of the political conflict between Czech nationalists and supporters of the Holy Roman Empire.

Jan Zizka was the military genius of the Hussites. He was 60 years old and nearly blind during the wars. Most of his troops were not regular soldiers but peasants and townspeople. For them he developed a new system of warfare, including the use of some frightful weapons and movable fortifications made up of armed farm wagons. Wave after wave of armies and crusaders from Rome, Germany, Austria, and Hungary were destroyed.

The death of Zizka in 1424 and the internal struggle within the Hussite movement marked the beginning of the end although the wars continued until 1478. The real danger which the German princes feared was not Czech domination but the influence of Hussite ideals. These ideals were greater religious purity and the reform of scandals within the Church. They also included ideas of greater social equality and political liberty.

After the death of King Wenceslaus IV, who had supported Hus, John Zizka led the Hussites in battle against the forces of the Holy Roman Emperor, Sigismund. Here, Zizka prays after battle. This painting is one of a series entitled the *Slavonic Epic* by Czech-American artist Alfons Mucha (1860-1939).

4. *Hapsburg Domination*

By the end of the fifteenth century the liberties of the Czechs were greatly reduced, first by their own nobles and then by the Hapsburg sovereign, Ferdinand I, whom they had chosen for their king in 1526. The Hapsburgs were rulers of Austria and fervent Catholics. They were more in sympathy with the Germans of Bohemia than with the Czechs. The intensive struggle between Catholics and Hussites, Germans and Czechs, was renewed. The Czechs were finally defeated by the Hapsburg emperor, Ferdinand II, at the Battle of the White Mountain near Prague in 1620. This defeat nearly erased the Czech people from Europe's history. For 300 years Czech independence was lost and its free institutions were crushed.

John Zizka defeated the Emperor in 1420 and 1422, but after his death in 1424 the strength of the Hussite movement diminished, and Sigismund was eventually recognized as King of Bohemia. This drawing of Zizka is by Czech illustrator Mikulas Ales.

The Battle of the White Mountain, one of the opening conflicts in the Thirty Years' War, had fateful consequences for the whole nation. This battle exterminated the Czech nobility. Over 30,000 of the country's leading families were forced into exile. There was destruction of life and property. Every house was searched for Czech books and writings. These were burned in the public squares to "eradicate the devil" of reformation. During the long years of war three-quarters of the population either perished or was exiled—a dreary monument to the Hapsburg dynasty.

13

Another band of Germans was then imported to settle in Bohemia and Moravia. German became the language of commerce, of the courts, and of all public transactions. The University was German, and in schools the native tongue was spoken only in the lowest grades.

It is worth noting that the Battle of the White Mountain took place only two months after the Pilgrims set sail for America in the *Mayflower*. Soon the Czechs were following this example and seeking refuge from persecution in the New World.

5. *The Nationalistic Reawakening*

Under Hapsburg rule, the Czech people were subordinated in all walks of life. They were treated as peasants, and their language was regarded as the servants' language. This treatment, however, helped to promote a certain unity among the Czechs. This unity was strengthened by the absence of class division, since the middle and upper classes of Czechs had been destroyed in 1620.

In the early years of the nineteenth century a literary and historical movement arose, led by the Czech historian Frantisek Palacky (1798-1876). Palacky's writings dignified Czech history. He regarded the Czechs as pious, peace-loving people who lived in a primitive democracy of equality. According to Palacky, the Czechs had fought the Hussite Wars for all humanity. They had struggled against authority and for the equality of men and freedom of conscience. Palacky felt that the Hussites had started the Reformation and had influenced the Puritan Revolution, which in turn affected the American and French Revolutions.

This interpretation made the Czechs the eastern outpost of the democratic and liberal West. It strengthened a patriotic spirit among the Czechs and helped direct them against the Hapsburgs and the Austro-Hungarian Empire.

6. *World War I and the Formation of Czechoslovakia*

One of the most colorful stories in Czech history is that of Dr. Thomas Garrigue Masaryk and his work to create an independent Czechoslovakian state. At the opening of World War I, Masaryk and several other Czechs worked in the United States, England, and other countries to help build support for the Czech cause.

Frantisek Palacky, Czech historian. His *History of Bohemia* emphasized the democratic ideals of the Czechs and their need for national unity within the Austro-Hungarian Empire.

In 1915 a Czechoslovak National Council was established in Paris. While the United States, England, and other Allied Powers battled Germany and Austria-Hungary, Masaryk worked diligently among the Allies. He visited President Wilson and worked with the American Czechoslovaks. In 1918 the Allied Powers recognized the Czechoslovak National Council as a government. In Washington, D.C. Masaryk proclaimed the independence of Czechoslovakia on October 18, 1918. Ten days later the Czech National Council seized power in Prague on the basis of the Washington declaration. The Revolutionary Assembly deposed the Hapsburgs, proclaimed a republic, and elected Masaryk president. Dr. Eduard Benes, who worked for Czech independence in France, headed the Czechoslovak foreign ministry until he succeeded Masaryk as president.

15

7. *Czechoslovakia Under Masaryk and Benes*

The new Czechoslovakia which appeared on the map of Europe in 1918 consisted of Bohemia, Moravia, and Silesia, as well as Slovakia and Carpathian Russia (Ruthenia), both of which had belonged to Hungary. Bohemia and Silesia had Czech-speaking populations. The Moravians used the same literary language, but their spoken dialect was a combination of Czech and Slovak.

The people of Slovakia were related to the Czechs through race and language. But the Slovaks had been separated from the Czechs for nine centuries. As part of the Hungarian kingdom, most Slovaks had become Catholics. A majority of the Czechs were also Catholics, but many did not attend churches. They felt strongly about the heritage left by John Hus and evaluated Roman Catholicism as a weapon used by the Austro-Hungarian Empire. Some Slovaks were unhappy to be part of Czechoslovakia and

Dr. Eduard Benes (1884-1948), scholar and statesman. He was foreign minister from 1918 to 1935, and then president of Czechoslovakia, heading a government-in-exile in London during the war.

Dr. Thomas G. Masaryk on a daily horseback ride from his official residence at the Hradcany Palace, Prague. Masaryk was president of the newly-formed state of Czechoslovakia from 1918 to 1935.

tried to retain their separateness. They even attempted to withdraw from the nation. This movement caused many problems for the Prague government. It also left its mark upon Czech and Slovak immigrants and expressed itself in the separate community relations of these people in America.

A United States postage stamp honoring Masaryk was issued in 1960.

All the provinces of the new Czechoslovakia, except Ruthenia, had been part of the original Czech kingdom destroyed in 1620. Ruthenia was formerly part of Hungary. It was transferred to Czechoslovakia in 1918 at the request of the American Ruthenians. Before World War I, few people had heard of Ruthenia, which existed only as an unimportant little corner of northeastern Hungary. The Ruthenians were without political rights and almost without education. More than half of the inhabitants were of Russian stock and spoke dialects related to Ukrainian. The rest were Magyars, Germans, and Jews.

Czechoslovakia and Central Europe, since World War II

Citizens erect barricades in Prague, May 1945. American and Soviet troops had already entered Czechoslovakia when Prague revolted against Nazi rule. Though 15,000 lives were lost, the revolt was successful.

The Germans living in the new Czechoslovakia played an important part in the developments leading to World War II. They comprised more than 20 percent of the whole population and controlled 40 percent of the industries, mostly in the area along the Czechoslovak-German border known as Sudetenland. Since they had been the favored element in the Austro-Hungarian Empire, they resented the new state. Eventually, many of them aided Hitler when he overtook Czechoslovakia in 1938.

8. *The Nazi and Communist Periods*

The Munich Pact of 1938, signed by France, England, and Germany, forced Prague to surrender the Sudeten region to Hitler. In 1939 the rest of Czechoslovakia was overrun by Hitler's forces. President Benes resigned and left for London and eventually the United States.

Under German rule the Czechs and Slovaks were executed and transplanted from their homes. They resisted bravely and profited from their experiences as fighters during previous centuries.

In 1945 World War II ended and Germany was at last defeated. Soviet troops took Ruthenia and then Slovakia. President Benes returned to Czechoslovakia and was re-elected president. Klement Gottwald, a Communist, became prime minister. Benes's policy of trying to maintain friendly relations with the Western Powers displeased the Russians. Finally, in February 1948 a Communist overthrow brought the country under Soviet domination. Thousands of Czechs fled to Germany's western zone and America. In June Dr. Benes resigned and was replaced by Gottwald, who transformed the government into a dictatorship. Since then Czechoslovakia has been under a pro-Communist regime.

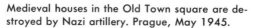

Medieval houses in the Old Town square are destroyed by Nazi artillery. Prague, May 1945.

A Moravian minister preaches to the Indians. The Moravian Brethren were noted for their missions, hospitals, and schools.

PART II

Czech Immigrants in the United States

A great deal of space has been devoted to the history of Czechoslovakia. This is because the long and complex story of the Czechs in Europe is closely related to the story of the Czechs in America . . . their reasons for immigration and their concern for their native country and culture.

1. *The Moravian Brethren*

As we have learned, the Hussites lost in their struggle against the Catholics and the Hapsburgs in the fifteenth century. The descendants of the Hussites, known as the Czech or Moravian Brethren, were among the victims of the Thirty Years' War. After the defeat at the Battle of the White Mountain in 1620, the Brethren, whose faith was based on the teachings of John Hus, were forced out of Bohemia and Moravia. They scattered to Slovakia, Saxony, Prussia, Sweden, Holland, and England.

The Moravians came to the New World because of persecution in Saxony. One of their leaders, Count von Zinzendorf, took steps to obtain refuge for them. He received a promise of land and free passage from the trustees of Georgia. In 1736 and 1737 Moravians arrived in this colony. Unfortunately, their wanderings had caused them to lose their identity. By the time they came to the New

The Single Brothers' House at Old Salem in Winston-Salem, North Carolina. The half- timber part was built in 1769, the brick addition in 1786.

World their names were so distorted through incorrect spelling that it is somewhat hard to trace their Moravian origin.

The Moravians did not get along too well with the authorities in Georgia, however, since they refused to bear arms in an English war against Spain. In 1740 George Whitefield, one of the founders of the Methodist Church, offered them a free passage on his sloop to Philadelphia. Thus, the first American Moravian colony was transplanted to Bethlehem, Nazareth, and Lititz, Pennsylvania. The Moravians also founded Old Salem, North Carolina. Many historical evidences of their influence are still preserved. The Moravian College in Bethlehem is one of the oldest American institutions of higher education, and the Moravian College for Women was the first such institution for women in America.

Although there were only about 2,500 Moravian Brethren in America by the time of the Revolutionary War, they were already known for their educational and religious activities. Many of the missionaries worked successfully among the Indians. They also provided religious education for many frontier settlements. Although they were pacifists, the Brethren served the American Revolution by allowing the patriots to use their general hospital and supplies.

The Moravians' greatest service was rendered through their Indian missions. Frequently, they persuaded the Indians to turn back from planned warpaths, and on several occasions they warned settlers of scheduled raids. They also cleared the forests, developed farmlands, and promoted education wherever they went, especially during the early years of white settlements in the Ohio country. Today, the Moravians retain only one Indian mission. However, they have a vigorous missionary program among the Eskimos in Alaska, and other Moravian missions are scattered throughout the world.

The work of the Moravian Brethren influenced American educational methods. Their communities in Pennsylvania had nurseries, boarding schools for boys and girls, and secondary boarding schools for older youths. In addition to the religious and regular subjects, vocational training was offered. Liturgies and hymns played a prominent part in the educational plan for children as well as adults. This emphasis upon the singing of hymns is widely felt throughout the Protestant world today.

The Moravians have, in fact, many religious and other "firsts" to their credit. Their spiritual forebears united to protest religious abuses 60 years before Martin Luther posted his 95 Theses in 1517. Moravians were the first Protestants to do missionary work as a church. Their religious ideas influenced such famous thinkers as John Wesley, Goethe, and Kierkegaard. The Moravians living in the Single Brothers' House in Old Salem had running water as early as 1778, and there one can still see what is perhaps the first steam table on which soup and other foods were kept hot.

Deep-well cooker in the Single Brothers' House, Old Salem. The unmarried men and boys of early Salem lived together in this house, cooked their own meals, and learned a trade. The building and nine of the craft shops have been restored.

2. *The First American Czech*

On Bohemia Manor along the Bohemia River in Maryland, there is a large brick house erected by Thomas F. Bayard, a United States Senator from Delaware (1922-1929). This picturesque home is located on the estate of his Czech ancestor, Augustine Herman (1605-1686), in whose honor both the manor and the river were named. Close to Bayard's home is Herman's grave, marked with the original stone which has been set in marble in order to preserve it.

Very little is known of Herman's ancestors and his early life except that he was born in Prague. In 1618 he and his family escaped to Amsterdam where he worked for the Dutch West India Company. Later he claimed to be the founder of the company's Virginia tobacco trade.

Herman engaged in trade with Brazil or Surinam, a territory in northeastern South America. He eventually built a large business in beaver skins in New Amsterdam and introduced indigo, a plant used to make a blue dye, on Manhattan Island. He bought large tracts of land in what is now New Jersey and with his partner, George Hack, became the largest exporter of tobacco in America. In 1659 Herman was sent to Maryland by Governor Peter Stuyvesant to settle a boundary dispute between the Dutch and the English. Charmed by this beautiful region, Herman applied to the Calverts for a large tract of land. In return he offered to make a detailed map of the entire area. The Calverts accepted, and the aspiring colonist spent 10 years surveying the shorelines and other boundaries of Maryland and Virginia.

The map, "Virginia and Maryland as it is Planted and Inhabited This Present Year, 1670, Surveyed and Exactly Drawne by the Only Labour and Endeavour of Augustin Herrman Bohemiensis," was as extensive and complete as its title. It was so well received that Lord Baltimore called it "the best map that was ever drawn of any country whatsoever." He rewarded Herman by granting him more than 13,000 acres of rich land in the extreme northeastern corner of Maryland, now known as Cecil County. There Herman built a manor.

Herman's vast holdings of land, coupled with his shrewdness and keen grasp of the conflicting claims of Baltimore and Penn, made him an important man on the eastern coast. He kept open house, with roaring hearth-fires and abundant meat and drink for visitors. In addition, he maintained a deer park and owned many slaves. This influential immigrant lived in great luxury until his death in 1686.

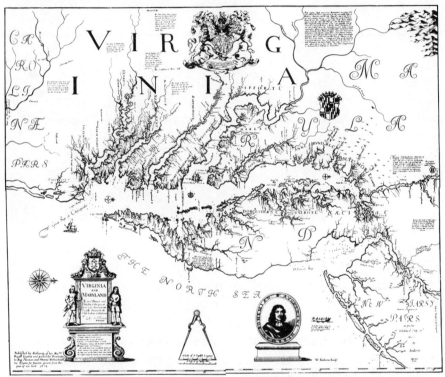

Augustine Herman's map of Virginia and Maryland, 1670, as seen from the Atlantic Ocean, designated here as "The North Sea." One of the notations on the map reads: "The land between James River and Roanoke River is for the most parts low, suncken, swampy land, not well passable but with great difficulty. And therein harbours tygers, bears, and other devouringe creatures."

3. *Mass Immigration of the Czechs*

From the arrival of the Moravian Brethren down to about 1840, only a few Czechs emigrated to America. Then a ravaging potato famine swept over Bohemia. Several Czechs left for Amer-

Bohemian farm women.

ica. In 1847, 39 soldiers deserted their Austrian regiment and left for the New World. This gave ideas to the others. One of them, Tuma, escaped to the United States with the regiment's money and invested it in a Bohemian beer hall in New York City. His letters to his countrymen were partly responsible for much of the later Czech emigration.

The real exodus from Bohemia-Moravia to the United States started after 1848. The number swelled constantly until 1870, and then again from 1890 to World War I. The greatest influx came during 1905 and 1906. The most serious causes of emigration were the poor economic and social conditions in Austria, combined with political persecution. Many emigrated to avoid being drafted into military service.

4. *The Attraction of America's "Pot of Gold"*

Once the immigrant landed in America, he was anxious to impress his friends and family at home. Many letters written by immigrants described the great opportunities to be found in America and encouraged others to follow.

The advertisements of steamship companies also encouraged emigration. Agents toured villages, telling of the golden opportunities in America. They were helped by the promotional activities of American railroads and state governments which were anxious to attract settlers to their undeveloped lands. Thus, large Czech farm settlements arose in Iowa, Wisconsin, Nebraska, Kansas, Oklahoma, and Texas. Today, in fact, Texas has more than 80,000 Czechs living in about 100 counties. Over 95 percent of them are farmers and live in communities where even the third generation still speaks the Czech language.

The first Czech farming communities were located in Wisconsin. The climate, though severe with long winters, resembled that of Bohemia-Moravia. The soil was suitable for raising maize, rye, wheat, oats, and vegetables, all crops with which the Czech farmers were familiar. Taxes were low, and one could become a citizen within a year. In addition, good land could be bought at $1.25 an acre. The Czech community in Milwaukee is one of the oldest in America.

Of the seacoast cities, New York was the only one to attract Czechs in great numbers, although for many years it was only a jumping-off place from which immigrants scattered inland. At one time St. Louis attracted Czech immigrants because it was the terminal point for boats sailing up the Mississippi from New Orleans. But in 1853 Chicago was connected with the East by rail. Travelers found it cheaper to reach the Northwest by way of New York and Chicago rather than by New Orleans and the Mississippi River. Chicago eventually became the largest Czech settlement in this country.

5. *Some Estimated Figures*

Determining Czech population in the United States by the use of census figures is subject to grave drawbacks. For many years the census did not deal with nationality, but only with place of birth, and its list of countries of birth was both incomplete and changing.

Bohemia was added to the census list in 1870 when it was still a part of the Austrian Empire. According to the census, then, Austria meant Austria apart from Bohemia. However, many natives of Bohemia claimed, quite correctly, that they were born in Austria. On the other hand, natives of Moravia still appeared as Austrians, although in reality they made one group with the Bohemians. For example, the importance of a large group of Moravians in Texas was hidden since the census figures combined them with Austrian Germans, Jews, Slovenes, and others.

At any rate, the 1880 census claimed there were 85,361 natives of Bohemia in the United States. The census of 1910 found 539,392 foreign-born persons of Bohemian and Moravian stock. The figures also indicated that most of these people lived in the Midwest, especially Illinois with 124,225. South of the Mason-Dixon line, Texas came first with a Czech population of 41,080, and Oklahoma second with 5,633.

The figures also showed that many Czechs were farmers, especially those who settled in such states as Nebraska and Texas. Others resided in towns, working at various trades. Czechs could seldom be found doing unskilled outdoor labor, such as road building. They preferred jobs in factories and shops. Musicians, both professional and amateur, were also numerous. Other Czech immigrants were employed as tailors, since many of them had learned the trade in Prague, Vienna, and Paris.

In each generation the four leading occupations were the same: farmers, general laborers, tailors, and agricultural laborers. In the first generation, many Czechs were tobacco and cigar factory operatives, carpenters, miners, and butchers. However, in the second generation, these places were taken by clerks and copyists, salesmen, machinists, dairymen, hackmen, and teamsters. Many of the Czech immigrants were saloonkeepers.

Although very few professionals were part of the immigration waves, the Czech settlements soon had their European-trained doctors. In the 1860's Czech lawyers appeared in Chicago, and later in Texas. Thereafter, aldermen and councilmen, school trustees, assessors, justices of the peace, legislators, county and town treasurers, registrars, and town clerks of Czech nationality increased in great numbers. Edward Rosewater, who was sent from Omaha to the Nebraska State Legislature in 1870 and 1871, was one of the pioneer lawmakers of Czech origin. Since then, there have been lawmakers of Czech descent in Nebraska, Iowa, Minnesota, Kansas, the Dakotas, Illinois, and Wisconsin. In 1904 a Republican from Chicago, Anton Michalek, was elected to the House of Representatives. Soon after came Adolph J. Sabath, also from Chicago.

After the formation of Czechoslovakia in 1918, the census figures changed again. In 1920 there were reported to be 362,436 foreign whites in the United States born in Czechoslovakia — 190,808 Czechs and 133,170 Slovaks. The census of 1930 stated that the foreign-born Czechoslovaks numbered 491,638. At the same time, there were 890,441 Czechoslovaks born in America. Therefore, the total was 1,382,079, or 704,271 men and 677,898 women.

The latest United States Census figures show that the following numbers were admitted to the United States:

1911 - 1920	3,426
1921 - 1930	102,194
1931 - 1940	14,393
1941 - 1950	8,347
1951 - 1960	918
1961 - 1964	616

These figures do not, however, include the refugees and others admitted outside the official quotas, as we shall see later.

The location of American Czechs can be seen from the figures of the persons speaking Czech in 1930:

Illinois	53,797	Pennsylvania	10,006
Ohio	21,820	Minnesota	7,814
New York	21,641	Michigan	7,440
Nebraska	13,839	Iowa	7,110
Wisconsin	11,254	New Jersey	5,200

A Czech restaurant in Chicago, center of America's largest Czech community.

6. *The Czechs in Urban Areas*

Like other immigrants, the Czechs who settled in urban areas formed colonies with their own people where they could speak their language, share advice in getting jobs, attend their own churches, and trade in the stores where Czech was spoken and where their specialties could be bought.

During the early days of immigration, the Czechs made their homes near the edges of cities, where they could have a semi-rural environment and enjoy their own gardens. After the 1880's, the immigrants came from more highly industrialized areas and settled in American cities where their special skills were in demand. In New York City they settled in the East River area and

Antonin Cermak, mayor of Chicago, was with Franklin Roosevelt in Miami on February 15, 1933, when a would-be assassin shot at the President-elect. The bullet missed, but it hit Cermak, who later died of the wound. This photo of Cermak is in the collection of the Chicago Historical Society.

spread northward. Chicago became the most "Czech" city in America and was sometimes called "Czech-ago." One of the city's mayors, Antonin Joseph Cermak (1873-1933), who was born near Prague, stopped the assassin's bullet intended for President-elect Franklin D. Roosevelt.

By 1920 the first and second generation Czechs in Chicago had reached an estimated 200,000. They tended to work in offices, garment shops, and at their own crafts rather than in large factories or other mass production industries. Many were in the lower ranks of the business and professional groups. Others owned grocery stores, saloons, and banks.

One of the urban areas greatly influenced by Czech immigrants and their descendants is Lawndale, a section of Chicago. Here Czech names predominate on shop windows. Czech motion pictures are advertised. Billboards and posters in the Czech language advise passers-by of social and cultural events. Even today, English is spoken with a distinctive lilt, and Czech is heard frequently. The community also has its own Czech banks, breweries, small factories, and meeting halls. Most of the single-family houses are one-story buildings in the architectural style common to Central Europe. They occupy very narrow lots, usually not wider than 25 feet.

Jindrich Feugner (1822-1865) and **Dr. Miroslav Tyrs** (1832-1884), founders of the Sokol movement.

7. *The Sokols (Falcons)*

The Sokol organization was founded in Czechoslovakia in 1862 by Dr. Miroslav Tyrs. Outwardly, the organization was a society for gymnastic training. But Dr. Tyrs hoped to accomplish much more. He wanted to keep the Czechs united while they lived under the Hapsburg regime. In addition to physical exercises and sports, Sokol members learned discipline and cooperation. Gradually, the organization became one of the greatest factors in helping to reunite the Czech people, socially and nationally.

Branches of the Sokol organization were transferred to the United States. There they became rich and powerful associations, owning gymnasia, libraries, halls, and magazines. The first American Sokol Society was founded in 1865 in St. Louis. In a short time, its branches spread to nearly every Czech settlement in the United States. Catholic Sokols and Workingmen's Sokol Unions also sprang up.

The Sokol Congress in Prague, 1938, drew Czech participants from all over the world.

Today the strength of the American Sokols is gradually weakening. There is less interest in the gymnastic classes due to the many activities competing for the free time of these people. The younger generation is more interested in the American system of competitive sports. A growing number of Sokol halls are facing financial difficulties. Their older members are aging and dying, and the younger members are attending in smaller and smaller numbers.

Czech-Americans march at the Sokol Congress. Prague, 1938.

8. *Churches*

Most Czechs and Slovaks are very religious. Their lives in America began in communities built around their churches, especially in the Midwest and West. The strangeness of frontier conditions and the inability to understand their neighbors' language and American political institutions drew the first Czech and Slovak families together. Because of lack of money, the religious meetings were held first in the homes of the members, and later in rural schoolhouses. When a sufficient number of families settled in the area, money was soon collected to erect a church building.

There were, however, many Czechs who seemed anti-religious, at least on the surface. Many political refugees formed "free-thinking societies." They built and supported schools for their youngsters in spite of opposition to their movement by such leaders as Dr. Masaryk. But with the liberation of Czechoslovakia and the passing of the "old generation," the movement began to die out. Eventually many dissenters joined Protestant churches.

Abbot John Nepomucene Jaeger (1844-1924) founded St. Procopius College and Abbey within Chicago's Czech community in 1887. Born in Bohemia, Jaeger came to America with his family in 1852. As a young Benedictine monk, he worked among the Slavs in Pennsylvania mining towns. Above, the library at St. Procopius College. The school moved from Chicago to a new campus at Lisle, Illinois in 1901.

Since most of the priests in nineteenth century America were Irish, the Czech immigrants who were Catholic made special efforts to secure and even import their own priests and to build their own churches. In fact, the only institutions of higher learning established by the Czechs in America were founded by Catholics: the St. Procopius College and the Sacred Heart Academy in Lisle, Illinois and the Notre Dame Academy in Omaha, Nebraska.

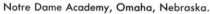

Notre Dame Academy, Omaha, Nebraska.

The Czech Catholic churches wove religious sentiments and ideas into the numerous Czech fairs, feasts, and national holidays. Christenings, confirmations, marriages, name days, pilgrimages, and national holidays all had the same gaiety as such occasions in the homeland.

Considering the fact that in Czechoslovakia the Catholics predominate, the number of Czech Protestant churches and congregations in the United States appears disproportionately large. Many Protestant Czechs are Presbyterians. The Czechs also belong to the Union of the Bohemian-Moravian Brethren in North America, and to the Baptist, Methodist, Congregationalist, Independent Reformed, and Reformed Congregationalist churches. The most famous of the Protestant congregations is the John Hus Presbyterian Church in New York City.

The chapel at Sacred Heart Convent, Lisle, Illinois. Abbot Nepomucene helped the Benedictine Sisters found this convent in 1895. His sister, Mother Nepomucene Jaeger, was the first superior.

The Czech churches in America honor many people who were historically important in Czechoslovakia. Most Americans are familiar with the Christmas carol about good King Wenceslaus. Wenceslaus was duke of Bohemia from 928 to 935. His chief aim was to live up to his Christian profession and teachings. Unfortunately, his cruel brother Boleslav lured him to a church festival in 935 and murdered him in cold blood. It is the anniversary of this incident that is celebrated as the Day of St. Wenceslaus. According to Czech legends Wenceslaus is not dead but fast asleep within a mountain in Bohemia, waiting to save his people in the darkest days of their misery.

To counteract John Hus's popularity with Czech masses, the Catholic Church canonized St. John of Nepomuk in the fourteenth century. Many churches in America are dedicated to his memory. Many Czech, Slovak, and Moravian churches are also dedicated to Saints Cyrillus and Methodius, the missionaries who first introduced Christianity in Moravia during the ninth century.

Among the several cultural functions which the Czech newcomer fostered was the drama. It was more than a means of entertainment; the Czechs wanted to be taught and inspired by it. Drama was an important part of the culture for Czechs living in even the most remote villages.

Dramatic groups became the earliest educational societies in the Czech-American churches. The pastors and school teachers functioned as coaches and directors in the production of several plays each winter season. For the youth, the play was a language teacher. For the parents it provided confidence and poise necessary in an environment where an inferiority complex was too easily acquired.

Parish choirs and reading circles were also an important part of the cultural life of Czech immigrants. In Bohemia, church services were accompanied by singing. The Czechs possessed hundreds of hymns and church chants, some of which were the earliest musical heritage of Bohemia and served as the source and inspiration for composers such as Dvorak and Smetana. Congregational singing was popular in the early pioneer churches. Later,

Statue of St. Wenceslaus, in Prague. The first great Bohemian ruler, he was duke of Bohemia from 928 to 935 and became its patron saint.

formal choirs were given the task of accompanying the High Mass and other solemn religious services. Some records show that masses were sung to the accompaniment of instrumental music.

9. *Efforts to Transmit the Cultural Heritage*

When the Czechs founded their parishes, they hoped that these would continue both the faith which they had acquired in Bohemia and the language, social customs, and traditions with which they entered the New World. But the same factors which have been altering the character of every national group in the United States have influenced the existence of the Czech churches. They are becoming more and more "Americanized," especially in the language of the services.

But values and traditions have a way of lingering under many different guises. Americanization has been, in fact, a surface rather than inherent quality. The immigrant of any national group naturally feels more keenly about Old World values than his children can be expected to feel. His inherited culture gives him a sense of self-possession and belonging, and helps to regulate his life. In holding on to old ways, the immigrant finds a door to escape the difficulties of his new way of life.

The Catholic fraternal organizations also helped preserve Old World values. They functioned in several different ways. As life insurance companies, they safeguarded the recent arrivals from poverty if the provider died. They granted support to members who were unable to work because of sickness or who were otherwise jobless. They assumed care for orphans and the aged. They built churches and represented the sometimes inarticulate Czech group in public and civic life.

In 1876 Saint John's parish of St. Louis took the first step to unify the many Czech fraternal clubs or lodges in the United States. The summons issued on September 17, 1876 produced a favorable response from 10 independent parish societies, which represented the Catholics in the more thickly Czech-populated regions: Chicago, Milwaukee, Allegheny (Pittsburgh), Detroit, LaCrosse (Wisconsin), Winona (Minnesota), St. Paul, Cleveland,

and Watertown (Wisconsin). The organization of the 10 still exists today as the Catholic Central Union. The pattern set by the Union was avidly followed in the 1880's and 1890's, the decades when Czechs came to America in great numbers.

Among the men's unions, lodges known as the "Cadets" or "Knights" were organized. These appealed especially to younger members who enjoyed military drills and formations, parades, band music, festive uniforms, and marches. Lodge members marched when a church was being consecrated or a rectory or school blessed. They accompanied church dignitaries visiting the parish for a performance of rites, and they became an honor guard to the newly ordained priest on his way to recite his first Mass.

The importance of the church in the lives of the immigrants can scarcely be overestimated. In other relationships, they were forced to accommodate themselves to American life. But within their churches they could retain European ceremonies, traditions, and language. The church was their place of refuge in the midst of an alien environment, an undisturbed corner of the old country in the midst of the new.

10. *The Czechs and Politics*

Before 1915 the Czechs in America had very little interest in politics. Individuals sometimes became members of a local political machine. In given localities where the Czechs voted as a unit, the entire group was repaid when one of their members received recognition by nomination to a minor office. At the same time, Czechs have been accused of being unusually harsh and critical of any of their group who attains a position of prominence or leadership. This attitude may result from centuries of national subjugation. Suspicion of political leaders undermined the ability of the Czechs to cooperate politically in their own country, where they were inclined to support ideals and causes rather than individuals.

Prior to the Civil War, because of their fervent stand against slavery, most Czechs were Republicans. They were also influenced by party organizations in their own ward, by family precedents, or by immigrant rivalries.

One of the first successful Czech politicians was a Democrat, Charles Jonas (1840-1896), a journalist who began his career as a member of the town council of Racine, Wisconsin. He was then elected state senator, and in 1885 President Cleveland appointed him United States Consul in Prague. The Democratic Party helped to elect him lieutenant governor of Wisconsin in 1890, and in 1894 Grover Cleveland appointed him consul general to St. Petersburg, Russia.

The political career of Charles Joseph Vopicka (1857-1935) began in Chicago. Brought up in Prague and educated in secondary and business schools, Vopicka supported himself by singing in the choirs of local churches. He then went to America and worked as a bookkeeper in a Wisconsin truck factory. A year later he moved to Chicago where he organized successful businesses in real estate, banking, and brewing. In 1894 Vopicka was appointed by Governor John P. Altgeld to serve as a Democratic member of the Chicago West Park Commission. He was also elected to the Chicago Board of Education. Shortly before the outbreak of World

Charles Jonas and **Charles Vopicka,** Czech-American politicians. Jonas was lieutenant governor of Wisconsin from 1891 to 1894, and headed American consulates in Prague and St. Petersburg. Vopicka was United States Minister to Rumania, Serbia, and Bulgaria from 1913 to 1920.

Captain Emanuel Voska (fourth from the left) with a group of Czech-Americans in Prague, 1919. Voska raised funds in America to help liberate the Czechs from Austro-Hungarian rule.

War I President Wilson appointed him Envoy Extraordinary and Minister Plenipotentiary to Rumania, Serbia, and Bulgaria—one of the greatest honors ever granted to an American Czech.

11. *The Czechs and World War I*

When World War I began, Dr. Masaryk left his country and organized a secret society in which the American Czechs took part to help liberate their countrymen from the Austro-Hungarian rule. An American Czech, Emanuel V. Voska, who was in Bohemia when the war broke out, undertook to raise funds from the Czech communities in the United States. From this source the finances of the whole liberation movement were mainly drawn.

Born in Czechoslovakia, Voska was exiled for his revolutionary activities. He landed in America in 1894 with four dollars in his pocket and with no knowledge of the English language. But by 1910, his marble-yards in New York City and Kansas City and his quarry in Vermont were well-known. He also became an American citizen.

In July 1914, Voska was sent by a committee of Czech journalists to visit Prague and report on the conditions of the Czech people in the Empire. He met Masaryk and agreed to organize American Czechs and Slovaks in behalf of their country's independence. Eventually he built up an amazingly effective espionage system against the activities of the Austro-Hungarian and German underground in America.

When the United States joined the war, Voska was commissioned a captain in the American Army and headed the Italian section of the American military intelligence services.

Before World War I the Czechs and Slovaks had not lived together in colonies or engaged in mutual activities in the United States. Since cooperation began at the time of the war, we shall now turn to the story of the American Slovaks.

The American Indian appears on a Czech postage stamp.

PART III

The Slovaks in America

1. *Who Are the Slovaks?*

Czech refers to the principal people or language found in Bohemia and Moravia. Slovak is the name given to the easternmost division of the Czech-speaking people. The supporters of Czechoslovakia, as one nation, claim that Slovak is merely a dialect of the Czech language. On the other hand, many Slovaks claim that they are an independent nationality with the right to form their own state, since their language differs markedly from the Czech one.

Most of these differences between the Czechs and Slovaks are due to events in history. Until 1029 the Slovaks formed a unit with Moravia. They were then torn away by the Magyars and isolated from the West. They were also forced away from the fertile farmlands and eventually repressed in every way. The mountainous environment of the Slovaks and their isolation and repression,

Slovak countryside. The mountainous terrain and lack of fertile soil made farming difficult — a major reason for emigration in the nineteenth century.

particularly since the early nineteenth century, hindered economic and cultural advance. However, the Slovaks have preserved much of their wonderful folk art and individuality, whereas the Czechs have become more cosmopolitan.

Throughout the centuries in which Slovakia was part of the Hungarian Kingdom, the Slovak culture was also influenced by the ideas of the Hussites, the Moravian Brethren, and Czech Lutherans. In general the Protestant Slovaks closely followed the development of the Czechs. The Catholic Slovaks, however, tried to create a written Slovak dialect which was separate from the Czech. This "separatism" between the Czechs and Slovaks in the "old country" has been mirrored in the separate organizations and aims of the Czechs and Slovaks in America.

Although Czechoslovakia officially united the Czech and Slovak peoples in 1918, both of these family branches have maintained a certain separateness in the United States. The Czechs reached America earlier than the Slovaks and had opportunities which were closed to latecomers like the Slovaks. Because of their better education, high rate of literacy, and political experiences in Austria, the Czechs became assimilated more rapidly in America than the Slovaks.

Vazec, a village in the Tatra Mountains, Slovakia.

Girl in Slovak costume.

Slovak peasants in costume. Czechs and Slovaks have preserved many of their folk arts — weaving, embroidery, and needlework — especially in the smaller villages.

2. *The Slovaks Come to America*

Before 1882 the Slovak immigrants to America were few and far between. In that year, however, these Hungarian subjects began to come in groups of considerable size. They settled mainly in the mining and industrial regions of Pennsylvania. Some found jobs in industrial Ohio.

The Slovaks' reasons for emigrating were mostly economic. Living in the north, they were able to make only a meager living on the land between the Danube and Theiss Rivers and the mountains. Because the Slovaks had to struggle for a livelihood, men and women were accustomed to hard work and a very low standard of living. Educational standards were also low. In most villages the schools remained open only five or six months during the year and attendance was rarely enforced. An average of 63 percent of the Slovak population could read and write, but individual counties had worse records.

In the 1880's the situation of the Slovak workers became worse. Unemployment was growing, wages were decreasing, and the cost of living was rising. The agricultural worker earned 25 cents a day. His staple foods in winter were only cabbage and potatoes. And the price of land was rising, partly because of the great amounts of money sent to these people from their relatives in America.

A further inducement was provided by agents of steamship companies who urged the peasants to emigrate. Labor contractors from America came to hire workers for the mines and steel mills. Many peasants who listened to the agents wrote back letters reporting high wages. These letters were undoubtedly one of the most powerful means of persuading the Slovak peasants to cross the ocean.

The Slovak immigrants usually went by rail to German or Dutch ports. The low cost of steamship crossing attracted many, since passage from Hamburg to America was only $20. The Hungarian government granted the Cunard Line the monopoly of transporting emigrants from Hungary. The rush to America was so great

Slovak immigrants arrive in New York. Most Slovaks left their homeland to escape from poverty. In the mines of Pennsylvania and Ohio they found working conditions poor and wages low.

that the Cunard Line called on other companies and formed the "Continental Pool" to handle the traffic. This "pool" provided the worst accommodations, the worst diet, and the worst navigation possible. The length of the journey varied from 15 to 60 days. The emigrants fortified themselves against seasickness with prunes and brought their own supplies of sausage, bacon, plum brandy, and gin. Water was distributed at intervals, sometimes only once a day. Ventilation in the living quarters was bad.

Most of the Slovak immigrants landed in New York. Others came to Baltimore, Philadelphia, New Orleans, Boston, and Portland. The problems of the immigrants did not cease when they landed in the United States, however. Often they were quickly parted from their meager funds. Hotels deliberately detained the immigrants by telling them that the train to their destination made the trip only once a week. Other swindlers met the immigrants as they came ashore.

To give exact figures on Slovak immigration before 1899 is impossible. Prior to 1899 the immigration authorities counted the immigrants according to the country of last residence, and many Slovaks listed Hungary as their country of last residence. After 1899 the immigrants were counted according to race or language. In the period from 1899 to 1910, the official figures show that America received 337,527 Slovaks. The peak year for the Slovaks was 1905 when 52,368 were admitted to the United States. In the 12 years ending June 30, 1910 Slovakia ranked eighth among the nations providing immigrants. The rate of emigration of Slovaks was 18.6 per 1,000. This was double that of any other race, except the Jews (18.3), Croatian-Slovenians (13.1), and South Italians (11.9).

3. Settlements

The Slovak immigrants who arrived in the United States usually went to the places where their friends and relatives had settled—the coal mining centers. The rest settled in the factory cities. One focus of settlement was the hard coal area of northeastern Pennsylvania. Before World War I, the mines in that district employed 75,000 to 100,000 men. Twelve percent were Slovaks.

Slovaks also went to the soft coal area of southwestern Pennsylvania. From there they moved northward to Latrobe or Greensburg or southward to Connellsville and Uniontown. Among the chief centers of Slovak settlements were such cities as Johnstown, Pittsburgh, Point Marion, Cannonsburg, and Republic. Only later did pockets of immigrants form in Chicago, Cleveland, and Detroit. Then, by 1885, large groups of Slovaks had also settled in New York, New Jersey, Connecticut, and Illinois.

Many Slovaks found work in the coal mines of Pennsylvania. These miners insert a dynamite cartridge after drilling a hole in the coal.

Until 1900 the Slovaks worked mostly in the local mines and at the coke ovens of the huge Frick and Company. The lowest paid worker in 1890 was the "yard worker" who earned $1.40 for a 10-hour day. The best wages were paid the "road man" who received $2.10 for 9 hours of work.

Some Slovaks were satisfied with their wages, which varied from $16 to $25 every 2 weeks. Strange as it may seem, it was possible to live and also save a small amount from these low wages. A pound of beef soup meat cost three cents. For six dollars a man could dress himself rather well. Rent cost three or four dollars a month for a small four-room house. Nevertheless, not all miners were satisfied and when the mine operators refused to raise wages, there were strikes, often riotous and bloody.

Loading a mine car with anthracite, or hard coal. Both photos of the mines are from the collection of the Pennsylvania Historical and Museum Commission, in Harrisburg.

Many Slovaks lived in "company houses," which were built practically at the site of the mines. These settlements of large houses were built by the company and rented to the worker who had also to pay for water, gas, and coal. To buy his food and other necessities the miner had to patronize the company store. This made the dependence of the worker on the company complete. The threat of expulsion during a strike was a powerful weapon in keeping the miners submissive.

The company rented a house to a married couple on condition that they take in "boarders," usually about 10 of them. In the larger houses, however, the number was as high as 30 or 40. The cleanliness depended on the character, ability, or sheer physical strength of the housewife. The food was purchased in common. One meal a day was eaten together, each weekday evening and on Sunday at noon. For the other meals the *gazdina*, or housewife, cooked whatever each man bought. Beer by the barrel was also bought in common—sometimes as many as 100 barrels a month. At the end of the month the common bill was divided. The housewife did not pay, but the men, including the husband, paid equally, and two children were counted as one adult. Moreover, on payday several barrels of beer would be bought as well as whiskey, and much meat was prepared for a gay evening. At first, dancing was the chief recreation. One man pulled out an accordion, and the dancing began. But any celebration—not just payday—was a good excuse for a long evening of dancing and shouting.

Family life among the Slovaks was weakened since many men came to America without their wives and families. They hoped to accumulate enough money to return to the homeland and buy land there. Thus, many crossed the ocean several times. It was only after several years that most decided to settle permanently in the new country. Some imported their wives, and others started looking for a wife here.

4. *Churches and Schools*

Most of the Slovak immigrants who first came to the United States were Catholic. Since they could not afford to build churches for their own use, they attended Polish, German, Czech, or Irish churches. If they happened to attend a church where Slovak was not understood, they often went a considerable distance to receive the sacraments from someone who understood their language.

The Slovak Lutherans were the first to organize a Slovak parish in America. A Slovak Lutheran church in Streator, Illinois was ready for services in 1884. Lutheran parishes were then organized in Freeland and Nanticoke, Pennsylvania in 1886 and Minneapolis, Minnesota in 1888.

The Slovak Catholics organized themselves at about the same time as the Lutherans. But they needed Slovak-speaking priests. In 1882 the Reverend Ignatius Jaskovic, the first active Slovak Catholic priest in the United States, came to Hazleton, Pennsylvania. He built St. Joseph's church there in 1885.

The Slovak Calvinists first organized as a religious group in 1887, although the building of churches did not take place until the 1890's. To conduct services in their parishes the Calvinists hired Magyar and English ministers. The Slovaks and Magyars fought about the language to be used in the services. There was no general solution to this problem, and the language used varied from church to church.

Since most of the original immigrants were hardly literate, many of them at first opposed the possibility of organizing parochial schools. They were interested in making money and looked upon their stay in America as only temporary. Why should they contribute to the education of other people's children?

A beginning was made in 1889, however, when the first Slovak Catholic school was built in Streator, Illinois. But there were not enough Slovak teachers, and many subjects had to be taught by English-speaking teachers and Irish nuns. To satisfy Slovak nationalists, the pastor taught children the Slovak language, history, and geography on Saturday afternoons.

5. *Organizations*

Economic and social needs caused the Slovaks to organize lodges soon after they formed larger settlements in this country. Mine disasters often took the lives of husbands and fathers, leaving their families destitute. To provide for sickness and funeral benefits, a large number of societies grew up in mining and industrial towns. The first was formed in New York in 1882. It lasted eight years, and Slovak was made the official language. Thereafter fraternal and mutual benefit societies mushroomed in the Slovak settlements. The chief purpose of these societies was to help those in need and to provide elaborate funerals. The secondary purpose was to help organize and build churches, schools, and lodge halls.

In the early 1890's the Slovaks began to unify their many individual lodges. This came about partly because of the rise of periodicals, a movement started by John Slovensky, a teacher from Slovakia. Slovensky came to the United States in 1879 and obtained a clerical job in the Austro-Hungarian Consulate. He was thus in contact with the Slovak immigrants who came to the Consulate seeking information about conditions in the "old country." This gave Slovensky an idea. In 1885 he launched a lithographed paper, the *Bulletin,* which contained news from Europe and items about Slovak immigrants. Tavern keepers subscribed to it for their Slovak customers to read. Success prompted Slovensky to embark on a larger enterprise, the publication of the *American Slovak News*. In 1889 a Catholic priest in Streator, Illinois started to publish the *New Homeland* and a year later saw the birth of two other newspapers, *The Slovak in America* and *The Bulwark*. These newspapers became sounding boards of popular opinion as well as a unifying force among the Slovaks. And discussion in the newspapers led to the consolidation of local lodges during the 1890's.

The consolidation of lodges brought new problems. The leaders could not decide if the principle of organization should be religious or nationalistic. The Reverend Stephen Furdek, a Catholic priest, believed that the new national organization should be based upon religious uniformity within the organization. He felt that Catholics, Lutherans, and Calvinists should each have their own organizations. Peter Rovnianek, a Slovak nationalist, wanted nationality to be the principle of any organization. He believed that any Slovak, regardless of religious views, should be a member. Because of this difference of opinion, two separate and somewhat rival organizations arose.

In 1890, Peter Rovnianek helped to found the National Slovak Society in Pittsburgh. All Slovaks were welcome. Openly nationalistic, the National Slovak Society played down religious differences, claiming that all Slovaks were one. The same year Reverend Stephen Furdek established a Catholic fraternal organization, the First Catholic Slovak Union. Its objectives were to preserve the Catholic faith, to support fellow members in need, and to preserve and strengthen the Slovak language and nationality.

The Slovak Lutherans organized their own beneficial society in 1893, the Slovak Evangelical Union. Soon after the Slovak Calvinists formed the Slovak Calvinist Union.

6. Recent Trends

Like other immigrant groups, the American Slovaks have had difficulty keeping their members loyal to Old World culture patterns, especially among the children born in the United States. In general, however, the Slovaks have been more successful in that respect than the Czechs. In 1965, for instance, the National Slovak Society celebrated its seventy-fifth anniversary. The First Catholic Slovak Union was in its seventy-fifth year, and the First Catholic Slovak Ladies Union, the Pennsylvania Slovak Catholic Union, the Slovak Catholic Sokol, and others were nearing that milestone. *The Slovak in America,* the oldest Slovak newspaper in America, was still in existence as was *The Unity,* official organ of the First Catholic Slovak Union.

The Slovak League of America has been active culturally and has published some valuable studies of the history of American Slovaks. The Slovak Catholic Federation of America has promoted good deeds in religious fields. The recently established Anton Bernolak Cultural Foundation is dedicated to the preservation of Slovak culture and literature by the printed word.

The politically minded Slovaks especially recall President Franklin D. Roosevelt's message to the American Slovaks during World War II:

> The country is mindful of the vast contribution the Slovaks have made to the cause of furthering the development and growth—moral, cultural and material. The stout hearted, clear minded, freedom-loving and determined people of Slovakia, who, sensitive of the wrongs and deprivations experienced in their own country at the hands of invading forces, turned to America seeking a new home, now compose with their children and grandchildren an asset in the life, industry and culture of this great land, that defies human power of appraisal. Evidence of Slovak devotion to the United States, Slovak enterprise, and Slovak influences, are to be found in all the States of the Union. To be able to avail myself of this opportunity of directly expressing my earnest greetings to the Slovak people pleases me unexpressibly.

PART IV

Refugees and Exiles

When Czechoslovakia was established at the end of World War I, there were over two million Czech and Slovak emigrants in foreign lands, almost one quarter of the number of Czech and Slovak inhabitants of the new state. More than 1,240,000 of them lived in the United States.

With the Nazi conquest in 1938 and with the Communist overthrow of the Czechoslovak democratic regime in 1948, another type of immigrant came to America, the refugee and political exile. More than 30,000 newcomers poured into the United States in the period from 1948 to 1962 alone.

A high percentage of these new immigrants were intellectuals and public figures. Their social and economic background differed greatly from the former immigrants who belonged to the lower and more impoverished classes in their homelands. These new immigrants represented their country's political and cultural elite. They were even more concerned with the possible liberation of their country and with the preservation of their country's culture than the former immigrants.

While the early immigrants usually came to the United States voluntarily, hoping to improve their lot, most of the refugees were forced to flee from their native land. Often they left their families, relatives, and possessions. Frequently they escaped across sealed borders. Some were shot at or hunted by dogs, while others lost their lives in flight.

Since the new immigrants are better educated than the original immigrants, many have had an easier path before them. They have been able to continue their professions and interests in America. But others have found the New World a very difficult place in which to live, especially at first. To be exiled, in flight, means to be homeless. The refugee enters an alien world at the very moment he becomes aware that his own world has closed behind him.

The exiled Czech and Slovak intellectuals were fortunate in coming to America during a period in which the American public was quite sympathetic to their cause. The first wave came when the Nazis overran Czechoslovakia. The second wave came after Jan Masaryk, the son of Thomas G. Masaryk, plunged to his death from a palace window in Prague. This happened a few days after the Communists took control of the government in February 1948. Masaryk wanted to maintain friendly relations with Russia and with the Western Powers and had thus kept his position as foreign minister in the new government. It is still not known whether his death was suicide or murder. However, the event helped awaken America to the danger of expanding Communism.

Many of the social scientists among the new immigrants have helped to meet the growing demand for detailed information about the past and present of Czechoslovakia. A glance at magazines and books about East European or Slavic affairs reveals the names of a great many of these men and women. Their scholarship, personal experiences, and knowledge of languages have greatly increased and enriched the fund of information available on this formerly "unknown" region of the world.

The effort which many of the new immigrants consider most important is the preservation and development of national scholarship. This is extremely important since the history of Czechoslovakia has not only been given a new interpretation by the Com-

Jan Masaryk (1886-1948) was foreign minister of the Czech government-in-exile in London during World War II, a position which he held when the government returned to Prague in 1945. He died shortly after the Communists gained control of the government in February 1948. This stamp honoring Masaryk was issued by the Czechoslovak National Council of America.

munists, but has been at times completely changed to fit the requirements of the Communist regime.

The Czechoslovak Society of Arts and Sciences in America was founded in 1960 as part of this effort. The Society has brought together Czech and Slovak intellectuals scattered throughout the world. Today it has over 600 members, mainly from the United States and Canada. College teachers, university professors, scientists, writers, and artists make up the bulk of the membership. The Society publishes a monthly bulletin which informs its readers of the activities of members and records their achievements. It has set up groups in New York, Washington, Boston, Chicago, and other cities which arrange social contacts among the members and schedule lectures and discussions. The Society has collected a small library and archives in New York and is preparing a "Who's Who" among Czech and Slovak intellectuals. It has also published a remarkable book, *The Czechoslovak Contribution to World Cultures,* which is an encyclopedia of information on the past and present life of Czechoslovakia.

PART V

The Impact of the Czechs and Slovaks on America

Most American historians have, until recently, underestimated the role played by those of foreign birth in shaping the history of the United States. However, the contributions made to America's heritage by immigrants is becoming more and more evident. This is also true of Czechs and Slovaks and their descendants whose achievements have lifted them to a level of national eminence.

1. *Science*

In 1896 Ales Hrdlicka (1869-1943), then a young medical graduate practicing in New York, went to Paris to study anthropology. After his return to America, he made numerous anthropological trips to Mexico and the southwestern part of the United States. The results of his trips earned him the appointment in 1910 as Head Curator of Anthropology in the United States National Museum in Washington, the first curator of physical anthropology in that institution.

Hrdlicka spent 40 years pioneering in the young science which he had adopted. He founded the *American Journal of Physical Anthropology* in 1918 and served as its editor until 1942. In 1929 he founded the American Association of Physical Anthropologists and made the *Journal* the organ of this association. Because of his interest in the different types of human skulls and his belief that significant changes were taking place in the size and structure of man's brain, Dr. Hrdlicka stirred popular attention. He found himself involved in many controversies, among them the issue of whether or not human life existed on the American continent in prehistoric times. He contended that man migrated here from Asia, through Alaska, at a comparatively late period. To support his

Dr. John Zeleny (1872-1951) and **Dr. Alois F. Kovarik** (1880-1965), physicists who taught at the University of Minnesota and at Yale University. Kovarik was born in the Czech community of Spillville, Iowa and received his Doctor of Science degree at Charles University in Prague.

arguments, he did much research in the Aleutian Islands, reporting his findings in hundreds of articles and in various publications. Dr. Hrdlicka earned many American and foreign honors. The valuable collection of skeletal specimens at the Smithsonian Institution is perhaps the greatest heritage left by this Czechoslovakian-born peasant to his adopted land.

Czechs were important in American universities as early as the turn of the present century. For instance, three of the Zeleny brothers, Anthony, John, and Charles, were listed in *Who's Who in America* and in *The American Men of Science.* Dr. Frederick George Novy, professor of bacteriology and director of the hygienic laboratory at the University of Michigan, was recognized as one of the foremost American bacteriologists and given the Cross of Chevalier of the Legion of Honor by France. Dr. Alois F. Kovarik was well-known for work in the department of physics of Yale University. When America entered World War I, he joined the United States Signal Corps and helped to develop devices to detect German submarines.

2. *Music and the Arts*

We can safely state that the Czechs in America have retained their love of music. In music they have probably reached their highest artistic achievement. Their impact can be found in many different forms of American music, from classical to modern.

When Old Salem, North Carolina celebrated the 200th anniversary of its founding, it presented programs of the Moravian Brethren's music, so important in the early community's way of life. American historians are only now beginning to recognize that tiny Moravian settlements in Pennsylvania and North Carolina produced an astounding quantity of good sacred music. The Moravians had published the first Protestant hymnal in 1501. The Moravian community of Bethlehem, Pennsylvania organized the first symphony orchestra in America in 1744. The Moravian Trombone Choir, organized in 1754, claims the longest continuous existence of any musical group in the United States.

Since the Moravian Music Foundation began collecting, cataloguing, and publishing early Moravian music in the 1950's, enthusiasm for it has spread to many other American religious groups. Choirs in other Protestant churches are gradually learning the 40 Moravian works published so far. Another 11,000 manuscripts lie unpublished and in many cases unedited in the underground vault beneath the foundation's headquarters in Winston-Salem, North Carolina. Thus, the Moravian music revival has inspired a wave of new religious music in the United States since the Moravians' 500th anniversary celebration in 1957.

Although he was not born in the United States nor did he emigrate here, Antonin Dvorak (1841-1904) must be mentioned in a discussion of American-Czech composers. Dvorak wanted to become the founder of a national "Slav" music, and based his symphonies and choral music upon Lithuanian and Czech folksongs. In 1879 his *Slavonic Dances* were already known all over Europe, while in 1880 *Slav Rhapsodies* spread his fame further both in Europe and America. His reputation earned him an invitation to conduct his works in the Albert Hall in London and to become a member of various societies and academies in England, Holland, Serbia, and Austria.

Antonin Dvorak, Czech composer who worked in America in the 1890's. He believed that composers should create a national music, with sources in native folksongs.

Dvorak then gained an opportunity to help foster a national music in the United States. In 1892, in order to encourage a native American opera, Mrs. Jeanette M. Thurber set up a "National Conservatory" in New York where free musical instruction was to be given to those who could not afford to pay. She offered the famed Czech composer a large salary to head this institution.

61

Dvorak landed in New York in September 1892. His ambition was to become the founder of American music, based on native Negro melodies which he found "ardent, fine, passionate, melancholy, noble, and bold." Dvorak's first step was to have Negroes admitted to the Conservatory, and one of the attractions of his concerts was the participation of Negro soloists and choirs. He began to put his theories into practice by arranging "The Old Folks at Home" and Foster's "Plantation Songs" for orchestra and choir, and by composing a cantata in four parts on the American national anthem *(The American Flag)*.

Dvorak was not particularly happy in New York. A Czech friend suggested that he spend his summer vacation in Spillville, a small Czech settlement in Iowa. There he vacationed happily during the summer of 1893 and there much of the famous *New World Symphony* was born. Although he was asked to remain in the United States, Dvorak decided that his place was among his own people in Europe. He returned in 1895 and continued composing until his death in 1904.

While Dvorak's compositions belong to the field of classical music, those of Rudolf Friml are well-known in the field of semi-classical music and light opera. Born in Prague in 1879, Friml came from a musical family who recognized his talent and encouraged him to develop it. At 10 he had already written a boat song which won the praise of his musical elders. Shortly afterwards he entered the Prague Conservatory for the serious study of music. When he graduated at the age of 17, he had attained such mastery of the piano that a joint tour of the European capitals was arranged for him and Jan Kubelik, a renowned violinist. In 1901 and 1906, Friml toured the United States, where at the close of the second tour, he decided to remain.

In America, where Friml was giving concerts and writing music, the composer Victor Herbert suddenly was unable to write a new piece for Tretini, a famed opera singer. Friml was called in to help. *The Firefly*, which he wrote for the occasion, was a great success. He was given contracts for more shows and music, and thus began a new and lasting phase of his musical career. His suc-

Young Czech-Americans dance the polka. This dance originated in Bohemia in the 1830's.

cess was repeated in *High Jinks, Katinka, Sometime, The Three Musketeers, Rose Marie,* and other light operas.

One of the most popular dances in Europe and America has been the polka. Although it seems to be related to Poland, the polka came from Bohemia. The dance was named in honor of the Poles who were great heroes in Bohemia after their uprising in 1830. In 1839 a Czech band which played the polka in Vienna attracted a large audience with its peculiar rhythm. The polka became popular in Berlin a year later and then in St. Petersburg and Paris.

The original primitive polka steps soon became complicated and refined. Solo performers did their best to add new steps and to make the dance even more difficult. Before long, Londoners became enthusiastic about the dance, and even the conservative Queen Victoria permitted it for one of her royal balls. The polka also popularized the peasant costumes of the Czechs and other Slav countries. Public performers, to impress their audiences with their foreign background, dressed up in whatever looked like a peasant costume.

The polka eventually crossed the Atlantic. In 1884, polka fever gripped the United States. Polkas were written for European audiences by Jan Offenbach and Johann Strauss, and their melodies were sung in America. Even today, polkas may be heard on radio and television. One of the memorable ones has been the "Beer Barrel Polka."

Rudolf Serkin, born in Bohemia in 1903, made his European debut with the Vienna Symphony Orchestra in 1915, and his American debut in 1933. Since 1934 he has made annual concert tours. He is also head of the piano department at the Curtis Institute of Music in Philadelphia.

Still other Czech-Americans have made important contributions in the field of music. Rudolf Serkin, a shy Czech-American, is a famous pianist. J. S. Zamecnik received his musical education in Prague Conservatory under Dvorak and composed the first music for motion picture accompaniment in 1913. Among his famous scores were those for the motion pictures *The Wings, The Rough Riders,* and *Old Ironsides.*

Jarmila Novotna made her debut in Prague as Violetta in Verdi's *La Traviata*. She sang at La Scala in Milan and in guest performances throughout Europe before appearing with the Metropolitan Opera in New York from 1939 to 1947.

Maria Jeritza and Jarmila Novotna are two well-known opera stars born in Czechoslovakia. Maria first became famous in Europe for her singing and for her beauty. In 1921 she was invited to join the Metropolitan Opera in New York. Jarmila Novotna so enticed the great conductor Arturo Toscanini that he arranged for her to come to America. Her work on behalf of her country during World War II was greatly appreciated by the Czechoslovak government, and her picture was printed on 100 Czech Crown money notes.

Maria Jeritza as Tosca, at the Metropolitan Opera, 1921.

Blanche Yurka, an American-Czech stage and motion picture star, appeared on Broadway as Queen Gertrude with John Barrymore in *Hamlet*. As Madame Defarge she was seen in the film, *A Tale of Two Cities*, with Ronald Colman. Her long career has ranged from the works of Sophocles and Ibsen to those of modern playwrights. Francis Lederer acted in the theaters of Prague, Budapest, Berlin, and London before appearing on Broadway and in American films. In 1958 he played Anne Frank's father in the road company of *The Diary of Anne Frank*.

Among American-Czech artists, Emil Kosa, Sr. is known both for his paintings and for his work in films at Twentieth Century Fox. Kosa's son, Emil Kosa, Jr., was honored in 1964 with an "Oscar" for his contributions to the motion picture *Cleopatra*. Josef Svak, an architect, designed the gothic pinnacles of St. Patrick's Cathedral in New York. Albin Polasek, when head of the sculpture department of the Chicago Art Institute, designed several busts for the New York University Hall of American Artists. His portrait busts are in museums throughout the United States; his *Woodrow Wilson* is in Prague. Mario J. Korbel, a sculptor known chiefly for his fountains and dancing figures, has a superb statue of St. Theresa in the Vatican.

Francis Lederer and **Vera Ralston** in the film, *Surrender*, 1950. Both are natives of Prague.

St. Patrick's Cathedral in New York City, from an early drawing. Architect Joseph Svak designed the gothic spires. European craftsmen decorated many portions of the cathedral, which was opened in 1879.

While we have noted here mostly Czech names, we should also record the contributions made to America by the Slovaks. Over 2,000 Slovak intellectuals left Slovakia in the last 3 decades to escape the Soviet armies. Among this wave of refugees are some of the best known Slovak novelists, journalists, poets, and writers. With the help of the Slovak League of America, they formed the Association of Slovak Writers and Artists. As a result of their efforts, several departments of education in the United States have included Slovak as a language course in their schools. It has been mostly in the educational and academic life that both Czechs and Slovaks have received recognition in recent years.

67

Conclusion

Only a few of the many outstanding American Czechs and Slovaks scattered in all walks of American life have been mentioned in this volume. But when discussing immigrant and refugee contributions to America, it is not adequate to simply mention the outstanding names. In fact, it is important to remember that there are hundreds of thousands of immigrants whose names will never appear in print. These people have contributed to America's history as farmers and as workers in coal mines, coke ovens, steel and rolling mills, blast furnaces, and slaughter houses. It is doubtful that a single steel structure in America has been built without the strength and skill of the Czech and Slovak worker. Thousands of acres of land in Texas, Wisconsin, Nebraska, Iowa, the Dakotas, Minnesota, and other states have been cleared and cultivated by Czech immigrants. Whether laborers or farmers, artists or shopkeepers, the Czechs and Slovaks have made a distinctive contribution to the diversity of American life.

A note on pronunciation:

No attempt has been made to indicate the pronunciation of Czech proper nouns, nor have the accents been included, though in most instances we have used Czech spellings rather than American or German variants.

ACKNOWLEDGEMENTS

The illustrations are reproduced through the courtesy of: pp. 6, 8, 9, 10, 12, 13, 15, 16, 17 (top), 19, 20, 26, 30, 33, 37, 43, 44, 45, 61, 66 Joseph S. Roucek; p. 17 (bottom) Post Office Department, Division of Philately; p. 21 Archives of the Moravian Church, Winston-Salem, N. C.; pp. 22, 23 Old Salem, Inc., Winston-Salem, N. C.; pp. 25, 67 Library of Congress; p. 31 Chicago Historical Society; p. 32 American Sokol Organization; p. 34 (top) St. Procopius College, Lisle, Illinois; p. 34 (bottom) Notre Dame Academy, Omaha, Nebraska; p. 35 Sacred Heart Convent, Lisle, Illinois; p. 40 (left) State Historical Society of Wisconsin; p. 40 (right) Department of State, Washington, D. C.; p. 41 U. S. Signal Corps Photo No. 111-SC-154762 in the National Archives; p. 42 Postovni Museum, Prague, Czechoslovakia; p. 47, 63 Independent Photo Service; pp. 49, 50 Pennsylvania Historical and Museum Commission, Harrisburg, Pennsylvania; p. 59 Yale University; p. 64 Columbia Recording Company; p. 65 Metropolitan Opera Archives.

ABOUT THE AUTHOR . . .

Dr. Joseph S. Roucek, a native of Prague, studied at Charles University, and came to the United States in 1921. As a student at Occidental College in Los Angeles, he supported himself by appearing in silent films and in vaudeville, traveling the western circuits during his summer vacations. He received his Ph.D. in international relations at New York University and has been a staff member and visiting lecturer at many American, Canadian, and European universities. He was professor and chairman of the Departments of Political Science and Sociology at the University of Bridgeport, Connecticut from 1948 until his retirement in 1967. Dr. Roucek has written numerous books, articles, and monographs dealing with the social and political life of Eastern Europe.

The IN AMERICA *Series*

We specialize in publishing quality books for
young people. For a complete list please write

LERNER PUBLICATIONS COMPANY
241 First Avenue North, Minneapolis, Minnesota 55401